Hip Hair Accessories

for the Crafty *Fashionista*

by Kara L. Laughlin

FashionCraft
Studio

CAPSTONE PRESS
a capstone imprint

Snap Books are published by Capstone Press,
1710 Roe Crest Drive, North Mankato, Minnesota 56003.
www.capstonepub.com

 Books published by Capstone Press are manufactured with paper
containing at least 10 percent post-consumer waste.

Library of Congress Cataloging-in-Publication Data
Laughlin, Kara L.
  Hip hair accessories for the crafty fashionista / by Kara L. Laughlin.
      p. cm. — (Snap books. Fashion craft studio)
  Summary: "Step-by-step instructions for hair chopsticks, clips, barettes, and other hair accessory crafts made from
repurposed materials"—Provided by publisher.
  ISBN 978-1-4296-6551-3 (library binding)
  1. Handicraft for girls—Juvenile literature. 2. Hairdressing—Equipment and supplies—Juvenile literature.
I. Title. II. Series.

  TT171.L395 2012
  646.724—dc22   2011002475

Editor: Mari Bolte
Designer: Heidi Thompson
Photo Stylist: Sarah Schuette
Project Production: Marcy Morin
Production Specialist: Laura Manthe

Photo Credits:
all photos by Capstone Studio/Karon Dubke; Shutterstock: vienkest (design element)

Capstone would like to thank Roxanne Guenther for her help in producing the projects in this book.

Printed in the United States of America in North Mankato, Minnesota
012012   006552R

Table of

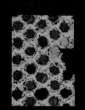
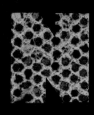

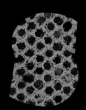

Feeling **Up** or **Down?**

Your hair says a lot about you. When it looks great, you feel unstoppable. When it doesn't, your whole day seems off. The projects in this book will help you through good hair days and bad. Whether you're dashing out the door or prepping for a party, your hair will meet each moment in style.

The directions in this book are only ideas. You might not have the same colors, fabrics, or decorations as shown. Don't worry! Let your inner designer create one-of-a-kind hair accessories your friends will envy.

Don't let the names of the projects fool you. Most of these projects can be altered to suit your personal needs. If you like the headband project but don't wear headbands, make it into a ponytail holder. If your hair is too short for a ponytail, try barrettes instead. Here are a couple more tips for switching things up:

- If you want to attach something to metal, use wire or thread to secure the item. Then use a touch of glue to keep things in place.

- Not sure what to do with your buttons, flowers, or beads? If the crafts have a hole, loop, or ring, get creative and turn them into ponytail holders. Slip the elastic band through the hole to secure. If the hole is too small, loop some wire through the hole and tie to the ponytail holder.

It's easy to change measurements to metric! Just use this chart.

To change	into	multiply by
inches	centimeters	2.54
inches	millimeters	25.4
feet	meters	.305
yards	meters	.914

envy—to want something owned by another

Hairpins, **Hollywood** Style

Hairpins are the shy girls of your accessory drawer. But if big screen romantic comedies are right about anything, all a shy girl needs is a little dressing up. Cue makeover!

You Will Need:

wire cutters
measuring tape
jewelry wire
hairpin
flower-shaped sequins
beads

Step one:

Cut a 4-inch piece of jewelry wire. If you don't have wire cutters, break the wire by bending it back and forth.

Tip: Line the edges of a birthday card with these hairpins for a great gift.

Step two:

Hold the end of your jewelry wire near one end of the hairpin. Wrap the wire around the hairpin. Make sure you cover the sharp end of the wire.

Step three:

Thread the wire through a flower and a bead. Hold the flower on the top of the hairpin. Then send the wire back through the flower. Turn the bead once to make a twist in the wire.

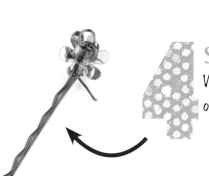

Step four:

Wrap the wire around the hairpin on either side of the flower.

Step five:

Cut the wire. Wrap the wire so that the end is hidden under the flower.

Bollywood Beauty

Brides in India wear ornamental jewelry called tikkas in their hair when they get married. But that's no reason to wait for your wedding. This red carpet style is just the thing for a semiformal. Or wear it to the cast party for the school play. This is one look that's made for drama queens.

You Will Need:

pliers

yardstick or measuring tape

15 inches of a lightweight
    necklace. Sections of chain linking
    beads together work best.

open jump rings

two spring ring clasps for necklaces

small beads

Step one:

Use pliers to separate a 15-inch piece of necklace. Be sure to leave a closed metal loop on both ends.

**Step two:**
Use a jump ring to attach a necklace clasp to a loop at one end of the chain.

**Step three:**
Repeat at the other end of the necklace.

**Step four:**
Use a jump ring to attach a single bead to the center of the chain.

**Step five:**
Add additional beads if desired.

How to Attach Your Tikka:
Pull your hair back into a bun or barrette. Catch a small amount of hair on one side of your head with the necklace clasp. Repeat on the other side of your head. If needed, secure with hairpins.

Sweet Thing

Ribbon-covered hair clips can be as sweet as cupcakes. But if yours look more kindergarten than cool, give them a grown-up twist. Make a pair for every day of the week, and keep your bangs still and in style.

You Will Need:

ribbon-covered
   hair clips
pencil
scissors
index card
1 small piece pink
   craft felt

1 small piece brown
   craft felt
1 small piece red
   craft felt
craft glue
glitter glue

Step one:

If your clips have bows on them, cut them off.

Step two:

 Draw and cut out a half-circle, a square, and a small circle on the index card.

Tip: Use a coin to trace the half-circle and circle.

Step three:

 Trace the half-circle on the pink felt, and cut out.

Step four:

Trace the square on the brown piece of felt, and cut out.

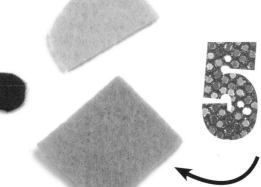

Step five:

Trace the small circle on the red felt, and cut out.

continue on next page

Step six:

Flip the pieces of felt over. Glue the red felt to the top of the half-circle. Let dry.

Step seven:

Glue the half-circle to the top of the square. Decorate the cupcakes with glitter glue. Let dry.

Step eight:

Use craft glue to attach the cupcake to the top of the clip.

❋ Variations:

- To make a skull, cut out a felt circle and square, and use a marker to draw eyes and teeth.
- For a patriotic look, go with white stars with blue stitching on red ribbon clips.
- Be sweet with strawberries by cutting a pink heart and green leaves out of felt. Use beads for seeds.

Chopstick Upgrade

Chopsticks are more than alternatives to forks. They can take the place of your ordinary hair band too. Twist your hair into a bun, and use these spicy sticks to keep your 'do together. This project transforms ordinary chopsticks from takeout to standout.

You Will Need:

acrylic paint and paintbrush
chopsticks
beading wire
wire cutters (optional)
10–20 beads of various sizes

Step one:

Paint chopsticks the desired color. Let dry.

Tip: If your chopsticks are too long, you can shorten them with a pencil sharpener. Sand down the sharp ends, and seal splinters with clear nail polish.

continue on next page

 **Step two:**
Bend the first 1/4 inch of wire back onto itself. Then cut a 12-inch piece of wire.

Tip: Safety glasses and gloves will keep your eyes and hands safe when cutting beading wire.

 **Step three:**
Place the wire on the chopstick about 3/4 inch from the top. The folded end should be pointed toward the bottom.

 **Step four:**
Wrap the wire around the stick two or three times. Make sure the wire covers the folded end.

 **Step five:**
String a bead on the wire. Wrap the wire around the chopstick two or three times.

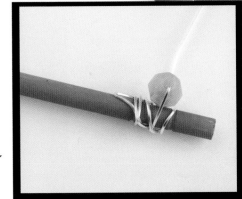

Step six:

Continue stringing beads and wrapping wire until you've covered 1 to 2 inches of the chopstick.

Step seven:

Cut the wire. If you don't have wire cutters, bend the wire back and forth to break it. Wear gloves to protect your hands. Tuck the cut end of the wire under a bead.

How To Wear: Slide the ends through braids or buns. Or use them to secure longer hair in a simple bun.

Gather your hair into a centered ponytail. Twist until the entire ponytail forms a tightly coiled rope.

Wrap the rope around itself, and tuck the ends underneath to make a bun. Hold the bun with one hand. Push the hair stick through the bottom of the bun until it touches your head. Then slide the tip of the hair stick out the other side of the bun.

Button Bands

Use your favorite fabric to make accessories that match your mood. Need a low-key look for gym? Pick a printed knit. Need to dress it up a bit? Try a scrap of embroidered silk. The metal loops on the back of the buttons, called shanks, will help turn simple buttons into flashy ponytail holders.

You Will Need:

large buttons with shanks
ruler
ballpoint pen
fabric scraps
scissors
needle and thread
ponytail holder

Step one:
Lay the button facedown onto fabric. Measure the distance from the shank onto the edge of the button.

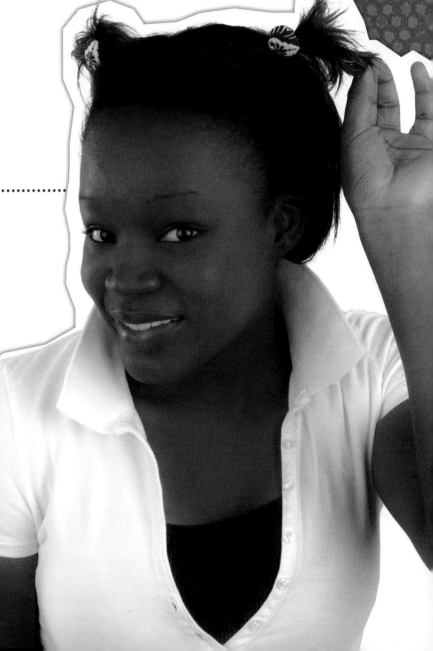

embroidery—a form of sewing used to sew pictures or words on cloth

Step two:

From the button's edge, mark the distance from step 1 onto the fabric. Draw a circle around the button. The edges of the circle should be as wide as the marked distance.

Step three:

Cut out the fabric circle.

Step four:

Stitch around the edge of the fabric circle. Leave a couple inches of extra thread at the ends.

Sewing By Hand: Slide the thread

through the eye of the needle. Tie the end of the thread into a knot. Poke your threaded needle through the underside of the fabric. Pull the thread through the fabric to knotted end. Poke your needle back through the fabric and up again to make a stitch.

Continue weaving the needle in and out, making small stitches along the edge of the fabric circle. When you are finished sewing, make a loose stitch. Thread the needle through the loop and pull tight. Cut off remaining thread.

continue on next page

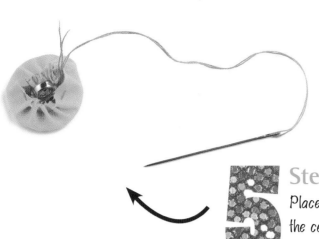

Step five:

Place the button upside down in the center of the fabric. Pull the thread tight so the fabric is snug around the button.

Step six:

Knot the thread. Make sure the fabric is tight around the shank of the button.

> **Tip:** If you're not a sewer, look for button-covering kits at the fabric store.

Variation:
- Glue jewels to the fabric for some sparkle.

Tip: Having trouble pulling the ponytail holder through the shank? Loop some thread around one end of the ponytail holder. Pull the thread, along with the ponytail holder, through the button's shank. Remove thread once the ponytail holder has been pulled through.

 ## Step seven:

Thread one-third of your ponytail holder through the button's shank.

 ## Step eight:

Thread the long part of the ponytail holder through the small part. Pull elastic out to the sides to tighten.

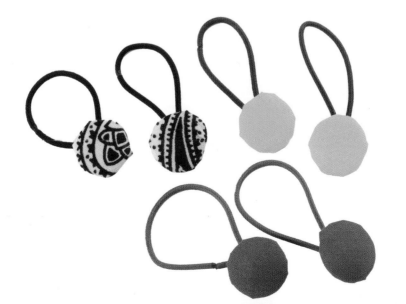

Beady Barrettes

Metal barrettes are boring on their own. But add some ribbon and beads and you've got an accessory as original as you. Give your hair a glamorous touch with barrettes decorated in metallic ribbon and silver charms. For a fun, flirty look, try pink and white ribbon studded with pony beads.

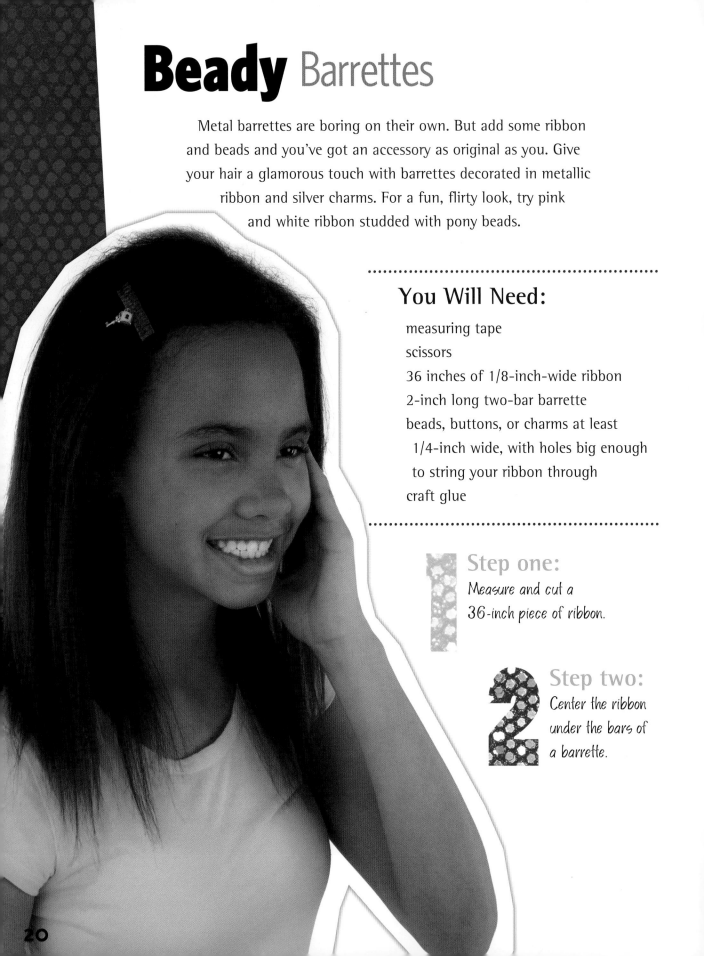

You Will Need:

measuring tape
scissors
36 inches of 1/8-inch-wide ribbon
2-inch long two-bar barrette
beads, buttons, or charms at least
   1/4-inch wide, with holes big enough
   to string your ribbon through
craft glue

Step one:
Measure and cut a
36-inch piece of ribbon.

Step two:
Center the ribbon
under the bars of
a barrette.

 **Step three:**
Thread the left side of the ribbon over the left bar and under the right bar of the barrette. Don't let the ribbon twist.

Tip: If you have trouble threading ribbon through your beads, dip the ends in glue and let them dry. They'll get stiff and act like a needle.

 **Step four:**
Thread the right ribbon over the right bar and under the left. Continue threading until you reach the middle of the bar.

 **Step five:**
Thread a charm or bead onto the left side of the ribbon. The bead should rest in the middle of the barrette.

 **Step six:**
Weave the right and left ribbons to cover the barrette beneath the charm.

 **Step seven:**
Continue weaving until the entire barrette is covered.

 **Step eight:**
Tie the ribbon beneath the bars. Cut the ends, and glue them in place.

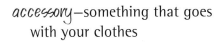

accessory—something that goes with your clothes

T-shirt Headband

If you find yourself running low on headbands, don't buy more. Make your own instead! Use a brightly-colored tee to really make a bold statement.

You Will Need:

T-shirt
scissors
measuring tape
needle and thread
pencil
self-adhesive jewels

 Step one:
Lay the T-shirt flat. Cut a horizontal strip about 3 inches wide from the shirt's midsection.

 **Step two:**
Measure the length around your head. Cut the fabric piece to that length.

 Variations:
• Cut holes in the fabric and weave ribbon in and out around your headband.
• Use glitter glue or permanent markers to outline your fabric's print.

Step three:

Flip the fabric upside down and fold in half. Sew the long end of the fabric together. (See page 17 for sewing tips.)

Step four:

Use a pencil to push the fabric through one of the short ends, so the fabric is right side out.

Step five:

Sew the short ends of the fabric together.

Step six:

Add jewels to finish.

Tip: If you're not great at sewing, use fabric glue on the headband's edges instead.

Garden Party

Give your hairstyle a sweet twist with polymer clay roses.
Go natural with pearly pinks and pale yellows. Or shake
things up with bright blues and eye-catching oranges.
Your hair will stand out with whatever colors you choose!

You Will Need:

polymer clay in any color, for flowers

scissors

green polymer clay, for leaves

toothpick

superglue

plastic or metal hair comb

Step one:
Soften the first
color of clay. Roll
seven 1/2-inch balls.

polymer clay—a type of plastic
that can be sculpted like clay
but does not dry out

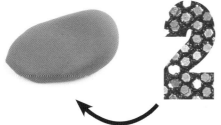

Step two:

Flatten one of the balls into a teardrop shape. The rounded part of the clay should be thinner than the pointed part.

Step three:

Beginning at the pointed part, roll teardrop end-to-end to create the flower's center.

Step four:

Flatten a second ball into a teardrop slightly larger than the first.

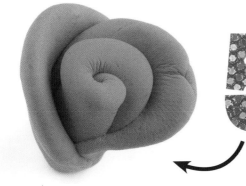

Step five:

Wrap the second piece of clay around the first.

Tip: You may have to blend several colors of clay together to get more realistic flower colors.

continue on next page

Step six:

Repeat with the remaining pieces of clay. Each new piece should be a bit larger and thinner than the one before. Make sure the pieces overlap. Gently roll the top edge of the petals outward to make the flower look realistic.

Step seven:

Gently press the base of the rose to make sure all the petals are attached. Use scissors to cut off most of the flower's base. Use your fingers to flatten the bottom of the flower, if necessary.

Step eight:

Soften the green clay. Break off two small pieces.

Step nine:

Shape green clay into leaves.

Step ten:

Use a toothpick to draw veins on the leaves and create a wavy effect on the leaves' edges.

Step eleven:

Gently press rose onto leaves.

Step twelve:

Repeat steps 1-11 until you have enough roses to cover your hair comb.

Step thirteen:

Ask an adult to help you cure your clay. Follow the directions on the clay package.

Step fourteen:

Use superglue to attach roses to hair comb. Let dry.

✱ *Variation:*

- For a marbled look, work a small amount of a new color into the main color until your clay is swirled.

cure—the process of baking polymer clay to harden it fully

Flower Girl

Go sweet with a flowered headband in your favorite colors. If you don't do girly, go bold by choosing brown, black, or even acid green for your fabric colors. Create a signature style, and go out with every strand of hair in place.

You Will Need:

nylon or polyester-based fabric, such as organza or taffeta
scissors
needle and thread
10-15 round beads about 1/8-inch diameter. (Make sure your needle will fit through the bead's hole.)
craft glue
small piece of felt
headband (any kind)

Step one:

On the fabric, cut out circles in three difference sizes. Cut out two circles in each size.

Tip: Use a gathering stitch to give your flower some ruffles. Use the sewing tipes on page 17 as a guide. Make your stitches long and loose. They should be about halfway between the edges and the center of the fabric circle.

When you've stitched all the way around the fabric circle, gently pull on the thread. The tighter you pull the thread, the more extreme the ruffles will be. When your circle is ruffled to your liking, tie off the thread and continue steps 2–5.

Step two:
Stack your circles from largest to smallest. Sew two or three stitches through the middle of the stack. End with the needle and thread on top of your flower.

Step three:
Thread a bead onto the needle. Push the needle back down through the stack. Add the rest of your beads the same way. Tie off the thread underneath the flower.

Step four:
Glue the felt to the underside of the flower.

Step five:
Glue the flower to the headband. Let dry before wearing.

strand—a small, thin piece of something that looks like a string

29

Glossary

accessory (ak-SEH-suh-ree)—something, such as a belt or jewelry, that goes with your clothes

cure (KYUR)—the process of baking polymer clay in order to harden it fully

embroidery (im-BROY-duh-ree)—a form of sewing used to sew pictures or designs on cloth

envy (EN-vee)—to want something owned by another

polymer clay (POL-uh-mur KLAY)—a type of plastic that can be sculpted like clay but does not dry out; polymer clay hardens when baked at certain temperatures

strand (STRAND)—a small, thin piece of something that looks like a string

Read **More**

Jones, Jen. *Updos: Cool Hairstyles for All Occasions.*
Crafts. Mankato, Minn.: Capstone Press, 2009.

Ross, Kathy. *Jazzy Jewelry, Pretty Purses, and More!*
Girl Crafts. Minneapolis: Millbrook Press, 2009.

Torres, Laura. *Rock Your Wardrobe.* QEB Rock
Your ... Irvine, Calif.: QEB Pub., 2010.

Internet Sites

FactHound offers a safe, fun way to find
Internet sites related to this book. All of
the sites on FactHound have been researched
by our staff.

Here's all you do:

Visit www.facthound.com

Type in this code: 9781429665513

Super-cool stuff! Check out projects, games and lots more at
www.capstonekids.com

Index